ALSO BY DAN CHIASSON

Where's the Moon, There's the Moon

One Kind of Everything:
Poem and Person in Contemporary America

Natural History

The Afterlife of Objects

Bicentennial

Bicentennial

Poems

DAN CHIASSON

ALFRED A. KNOPF   NEW YORK   2014

THIS IS A BORZOI BOOK

PUBLISHED BY ALFRED A. KNOPF

Copyright © 2014 by Dan Chiasson

Library of Congress Cataloging-in-Publication Data
Chiasson, Dan.
Bicentennial : poems / Dan Chiasson.—First edition.
pages cm
ISBN 978-0-385-34981-9 (hardback) ISBN 978-0-385-34982-6 (eBook)
I. Title
PS3603.H54B53   2014
811'.6—dc23   2013027872

Front-of-jacket photograph © Jens Mortensen/Galeries/Corbis
Jacket design by Carol Devine Carson

Manufactured in the United States of America
First Edition

For Louis and Nicholas, again

I go up but at the same time I go down.
Present tense I am; but past tense too.
Three is one too many, one is one too few.

—OLD RIDDLE

Contents

1.
One on One

2.
Arm in Arm

3.
Bicentennial

1.

One on One

Overtime

In this alternate basketball nobody plays,
Both players try to tie the score:
That way, at the buzzer, the game isn't over.

Look, a show of courtesy: the winning player
Is helping the loser score, the way
Our youths assist the cold, suffering elderly.

Or here, a boy is helped to understand
The exotica of his changing body:
When X turns to Y you do not die;

When Y turns to Z we call it joy;
This process crests until someday
You fall off the edge of the alphabet.

The players play even when they do not play;
See, in just this way, we grow old
Alongside the returned jays and fat magnolias;

The game goes on forever this way, the players
Suspended in infinite overtimes,
The score climbing in never-changing change—

Until the day the backboard shatters
And the blackboard blossoms
With arcane formulae and blackbird wings.

Away We Go

Little bird, little sugar cube,
Tell me all the state secrets
Of the crab apple, barberry, brake,
The concealed locales, the plots

Only you can unravel, my figurine,
O my collectible dinnerware,
I've hunted everywhere for answers;
Answer me, my New Jersey kingpin,

My flower hoarder, electronic eye,
My windup mini-Frankenstein;
If I speak into your corsage,
And say it slowly, so we both nod off:

My father died, nor was he at the height
Of his career as a bowler, nor
Had he discovered the cure for NASCAR—
Quite without fanfare, little jackass,

O my severely damaged little friend,
He died, and what I felt, pea pod,
Projection, tired device, was shy:
Surely you can identify, flight risk,

Going from unconscious whim to whim
As though the forest was only scenery?
I settle for thick yogurt, bird,
While you get to eat the scenery.

I'm one of the whims, fatherless
In this brand-new way, observing as
My father's features idle inside
And thicken my sons' cheekbones:

Where did you come by your business casual,
Your sturdiness and eerie sobriety
Auditing the Spring's enormous income
While I piss my windfall zilch away?

Obituary

Dawn awoke and rose one person down that day.
Across the Universe, the obituary and I
Engulfed a granola and yogurt parfait.

I found my focus in his rifle's sights.
I was crossed out in the list
Of his next of kin, in Halifax black-and-white.

He bowled frame upon frame of erect Jesuits.
He changed his name. He synchronized Christ
With deep time, a paleontologist turned priest.

He taught the Inuit not to shiver or shout
When they enunciated pure Canadian:
They traded their own pelts for the cool ESL.

He flew to Seoul, to the reggae gymnasium,
To the icebreaker mojito outing,
To twin Filipinas with my features.

I stood sentry and watched my own reentry
Expecting a theft, never expecting
To witness myself absconded when I absconded,

Both looter and loot, at night, on foot . . .
What happens to me now, no one can say:
When the sun breaks now it just breaks even;

Somewhere the cockcrow cul-de-sac *alarum* sounds;
The curtain falls and so concludes
My offensive, possibly illegal vaudeville act.

One on One

It is the nature of this game to want possession
Then to want to give it up
To get it back so you can give it up again.

Nobody stops to ponder the ball, the way John Keats
Pondered a cue ball's "roundness,
Smoothness, volubility": its joy in being hit.

Imagine the score is tied, and I take the ball away
In order to sketch it, or incorporate it
Into some kind of quasi-tribal dance routine . . .

I thought we had agreed to play. I thought you said
We'd play and play all day, beating and being beaten,
Taking turns at losing, learning its advantages

For a young man's character, then changing fates.
What kind of game is this, your going away forever,
Sending word, years later, that you'd died?

2.

In high school we had parties in the woods
In the winter, and we rode snowmobiles
Higher and higher until we were high enough

Nobody could see any sign of our fire.
If there was a girl you liked, you sort of
Nuzzled up beside her, if that was her,

If that was even a girl. It was hard to tell
In the dark, in our gigantic parkas,
Who was who. You had to make a guess

Based on factors extremely difficult to discern
In the wind, by a sputtering fire, and
Sometimes you cuddled the hockey captain.

3. TITIAN V. ROAD RUNNER

If you are made for flight, intended for it,
You had better find a pursuer, fast.
Otherwise all that fleeing is going nowhere.

This bull, he's got a bad intent, he wants
To hog the entire corner of the picture.
The girl is looking tasty to the espying putti.

This small bird crisscrossing my childhood
At enormous speed, outrunning everything,
Running out of road to run down, running

Out of canyon, running out of cartoon
Runs out of the cartoon, never to return.
That's why this landscape looks forlorn.

4. TACKLE FOOTBALL

Snow up to our waists and coming down still.
There was a field here once, when we began.
We marked the end zones and set up the goals.

Now nobody can even move, much less tackle.
I am Ganymede fleeing on a temple frieze.
We stand around like lovesick Neanderthals.

We're Pompeian before Pompeii was hot.
We have the aspect of the classic dead
Or of stranded, shivering astronauts.

It was early in the era of the pause button:
We paused and paused the afternoons away
Indoors, blasting our ballistic erections

At the blurred bikinis of celebrities,
Then, splaying on the linoleum floor,
Awaited the apportioned pizza delivery.

Now, someone has paused us, or so it appears,
But they didn't pause the snow, or the hour:
As the one gets higher, the other gets later.

5.

I might have been John Keats, for all you knew.
I still could be: it's not impossible.
For several years John Keats was not John Keats.

So say I was John Keats, and you'd gone to Alaska.
Odd choice you made, preferring snow to poetry.
The point is to stick around on the slender chance

A person's son turns into a canonical writer.
The point is not to shiver on the horizon
And correct an Inuit's prepositions.

I was tiny to you, like all things far away.
But you were tiny too, and plus, you were cold.
You look like a bumblebee in your tiny snowsuit.

The Donkey

This time around, we start out in the clouds.
Look down: our ceiling is plush carpeting.
An elderly Kenyan beside us is praying.
She gets out her missal and silently reads.

The donkey bore our Christ upon his back
And yet this beast is not respected,
Nobody tells how bravely he acted.
Let that be the subject of your book.

The donkey, he is the noblest of beasts
(Says this woman to me, when I tell her
I work as a writer and a teacher):
Why people do show him this disrespect?

Then she turns back to her small red missal.
Occasionally I hear her whisper Amen.
Her son sets out now to meet her in Boston.
I am watching the big screen in the aisle,

Where you and I, the woman, and everyone
Crawl like a housefly across the screen
Inside a tiny icon of the plane we're on,
More real to ourselves as a representation,

All of us going west inside the circuitry
That guides the plane across continents,
And guides the icon plane across the screen,
Riding that circuitry like a superstrong donkey.

So, tell everyone, when you put down my book:
The donkey is the noblest of beasts,
For he bore on his back the suffering Christ,
And never once wavered, nor shuddered, nor broke.

Inscription

Things traced by what they trace: the flashlight,
Not the slingshot . . . as though to orbit was the point.

As though going round and round reiterating
Were a form of argument; the way a globe is spun;

The way, cleaving the air, the boomerang must zip
Whatever it unzipped, the carousel horse gallop

Idiotically to its tune, its smile painted on.
As though a beat was an adventure. The insufficient margin.

The margin in all things makes them too valuable to be
Any value at all, the inscription *To Chester, from Wystan*

That surplus in the chastity, *To Chester;* a line
Ruining, by embodying it, its potential power;

Remembered looking forward, as though not one minute more
On the planet won't be, and it won't be, the undoing

Of everything I did, the boomerang returning, its limit shot,
From Wystan, its limit never met, the horizon near

My body worn as a light sweater, something thrown on
On a cold night, getting colder, near the end of summer.

The Flume

Here we go up again, up again, the mountain
The men who have assembled it for years
Assembled yesterday, so that you and I

Headed who knows where together, but
Headed there together, will see
From the top the bottom, from the bottom the top,

Then feel the inside-outside-all-over-nowhere
My God I Am Going to Die, Not Someday, Now
Sensation that, once we plateau, feels silly,

Since when were we safer than when we sought
The danger that when it subsided returned
Us to the dangers it had blotted out?

There are no fears, here at the start:
This is when, the book just opened,
Knowing you will one day know the story

You don't know yet changes the story
You are getting to know, the way we know
Before we know what anything means it means

Something: a fireworks display, the birthday
Of the Country; that's me; my uncle and I
Are racing through the past on the Python,

Which men assembled absentmindedly that day
And, so you could visit it with me,
I assembled here again inside my memory;

Now, when you remember how things were
Today, you will also remember yourself
Looking forward to yourself looking back,

A looking back that, here in your past,
You do already, you already say
About what happened yesterday, remember when . . . ?

—The future doing its usual loop-de-loop,
The sons all turning into fathers
Until the absentminded men take the ride down.

Star Catcher

We felt like dying when the Yankees won.
In 1979, they seemed to win all summer.
Our luck changed when the plane went down.

My friend was born because his brother drowned.
We rode robin's egg bikes alongside each other.
We felt like dying when the Yankees won.

Time, that is huge at the start of the season,
By August grows smaller and smaller;
The clock stopped when the plane went down.

The logic of loss, we could all understand:
Every fan trusts that losing is barter.
Though we wanted to die when the Yankees won,

We knew that all losers eventually win,
Every drowned brother results in another:
As the plane goes, so goes Thurman Munson.

Now Tommy John, Ron Guidry, and the whole rotation,
Whenever they pitched would pitch to air.
The star catcher was gone. Even if the Yankees won,
They'd lost their catcher, their star: Thurman Munson.

Interviewing Janet Malcolm

To interview the interviewer, you need a mirror.
She's trading privacy for peekaboo.
Janet Malcolm writes the questions that she answers.

Her apartment had the air of "New York Writer":
The cat, the glass-top table, a park view;
On the far wall, facing us, an ornate mirror.

Her cat, and not her id, caused the disorder;
(This poem is partly false and partly true);
Janet Malcolm writes the questions that she answers.

The cat was just one detail in the picture.
The table was classic Mies van der Rohe.
Outside, the reservoir was a big mirror.

That day my objectivity danced with hers,
Our "journalistic egos" locked in tango,
She rewrote the questions she had answered.

She'd interviewed herself, I realized later;
I was bystander to a rendezvous.
I stared at my reflection in the mirror.
Janet Malcolm changed the questions she had answered.

Nowhere Fast

1.

Give me your secret.
I can keep it.
I'll become it.

2.

The way ski racers
Lining up
Become the race:

3.

Look what was put
Into the pot
And what came out!

4.

The way each choice
That made itself
Make us unmade us;

5.

Hid us, betrayed us.
O my compass
Your wilderness

6.

Awaits reply:
Say you and I
Will find our way

7.

Eventually—
Like see and saw,
Or sea and sky.

Cosmonaut and Newsboy

Under the illustration it says I say
Something about the length of his journey
And something about the length of his stay
Before we commence with the day's activity:
He is to come upstairs and comfort me.
He does not want this and neither do I.
But it says so in a caption we both see
And can both see that the other sees.
We shrug our shoulders and we make our way.
I make an awkward joke. He laughs awkwardly.
We are captive to what happens in the story.
In the white space between lines, we obey.
We have dressed, according to the story,
(Which feels now like cruel parody)
Each as the other saw him in his mind's eye:
I am wearing my newsboy suit, and he
Is dressed as a cosmonaut. And this is why,
Though we are strangers, this man and I,
A cosmonaut snuggling a newsboy,
Happily we snuggle the day away.

Opening Lines

1.

A shovel meets a hole in a bar:
Don't I know you from somewhere?
An implosion runs into a star:
Darling, what's the matter?

2.

The boy in the Egyptian wing
Wanted one thing:
For his father
To lift him over
The glass case
Where the sarcophagus
For a century
Lay empty,
The bones and treasures
Sold to collectors,
And to pretend
Again and again
To lower him in.

3.

When a tool outlives its use, the destruction
It wrought is wrought on it, in slow motion,
By time. And so it suffers its own function,

Until someone invents the idea of history,
And someone else, the idea of beauty,
And someone else, the idea of money,

And the process of ruin that time began
On the tool is slowed, though not undone,
By fund-raisers and by a capital campaign.

4. OPENING LINES

When we drove in the car to see the carnage
And bushwhacked as fast as we could manage
We still had to wait at the end of the trail
For the train we came to see derail.

5.

In my dream, I broke into the museum at night
And freed the birds first, and they flew,
And freed the massive cats, who strode,
And freed the fleet stags, who darted,
And freed the low-slung reptiles, and swarms
Of metallic insects and, best, butterflies;

Every creature returned to his element!
The cases flew open and motion returned.
It was alpha and omega tangoing.
But I had no water for the fish,
And I had no flesh for the bones
Of the giant whale that hangs in the hall;
And I had no time, so I left the mastodon alone.

6. 2001

As I explained to my children, the future
This movie imagines is now in the past.
They understood this perfectly;
The future happened before they were born;
And the past, as they innately understand,
These names they hear, Rome, Napoleon—
This they learn later, all of this
They know will happen in the future.

7. LULLABY

Oh, all the stars, and the Big Dipper,
And their reflections in the ocean:
It doesn't matter, it doesn't matter;

And the creatures, their weird behaviors,
Some made to thrive, and some to die;
Part of their natures, part of their natures;

It doesn't matter, it happens later:
All of creation, the seven days,
The famous storm, the rainbow after;

One day the cardinal, he wakes up red;
One day the jay realizes why
Of all the creatures, he got his color:

This happens later, tonight, good night.
When someone wins, somebody loses:
Something is ravaged, something is fed;

All of history, even the Romans,
They happen later, tonight sleep tight.
You'll learn this later. Tonight, good night.

And all desire, and every setback,
These happen later, happen much later;
Tonight it's late, tonight it's late.

You could stay up, but then the past
Would just be longer, be that much longer;
Sleep will take care of the extra hours.

You'll learn it later. It happens later.
The gains we made, they'd be erased,
By another day, another day:

Tonight you're sleepy, so close your eyes.

8. OPENING LINES

All the meanings are already taken,
And so the words, forsaken
Wander in the woods and pine.
Little poem of mine: what's your sign?

Father and Son

Only much later did they see, the two of them,
That never knowing one another, there was nothing

Not to know; that not being to begin with meant
Those later, more drastic negations negated nothing;

This was to be the poignant part of it: nothing
Nevertheless would someday end; and the wish—

He wished it in a priory, he wished it in a mall—
Was that when nothing ended it might be

If not an event, at least not a nonevent.
Which, in the end, when it happened, it wasn't.

Vital Signs

The moon in a manuscript,
A man on a monument,
A tree on a tapestry:

Everything valuable
Hidden away;
Everything visible
Visibly empty.

I turned the pain up
In my poetry,
And now the beat won't stop:

The ticktock of the lunatic,
The man in the manslaughter,
The moose in the museum.

2.

Arm in Arm

Echolalia: A Play in Ten Acts

I.

CHILD A enters, holding a bouquet of orange peonies.

II.

CHILD B enters, holding a bouquet of orange peonies.
CHILD A draws a boat he labels "Boat Inside a Dream."

III.

CHILD C enters, holding a bouquet of orange peonies.
CHILD B draws a boat he labels "Boat Inside in a Dream."
CHILD A rewires a radio to hear how the song goes.

IV.

CHILD D enters, holding a bouquet of orange peonies.
CHILD C draws a boat he labels "Boat Inside a Dream."
CHILD B rewires a radio to hear how the song goes.
CHILD A hikes down the North slope to see June snow.

V.

CHILD E enters, holding a bouquet of orange peonies.
CHILD D draws a boat he labels "Boat Inside a Dream."
CHILD C rewires a radio to hear how the song goes.
CHILD B hikes down the North slope to see June snow.
CHILD A stands in a garden on the first of June. He finds the
    brightest orange peony.

VI.

CHILD F enters, holding a bouquet of orange peonies.
CHILD E draws a boat he labels "Boat Inside a Dream."
CHILD D rewires a radio to hear how the song goes.
CHILD C hikes down the North slope to see June snow.
CHILD B stands in a garden on the first of June. He finds the
    brightest orange peony.

VII.

CHILD F draws a boat he labels "Boat Inside a Dream."
CHILD E rewires a radio to hear how the song goes.
CHILD D hikes down the North slope, the dark slope, the steep
    slope, the slope sick sorrow took, to see June snow.
CHILD C stands in a garden on the first of June. He finds the
    brightest orange peony.

VIII.

CHILD F rewires a radio to hear how the song goes.
CHILD E hikes down the dark slope.
CHILD D stands in the garden on the first of June. He finds
the brightest orange peony.

IX.

CHILD F hikes down the slope sick sorrow took. He finds the
whitest June snow.
CHILD E stands in the garden on the first of June. He finds the
brightest orange peony.

X.

CHILD F decides to write a book. To be in the book, you have
to pick a flower.
Since he picked a flower, he must be in the book.
Since you are in the book, you must have picked a flower.

The Ferris Wheel in Paris: A Play

Dramatis Personae

A MAN

A FAERIE

*

(An empty stage. MAN stands at the front of the stage.)

MAN:

There would have to have been, first, something:
First darkness, then a stage;
Then an actor and an audience;
There must have been a single play,
And then the idea of theater,
And the human drive to be entertained,
And before that, just to be happy;
Curiosity about this category, "human,"
Must have been prior, must have been ancient.
For a faerie to appear there had to be faeries,
For her to say my name and I was there,
Standing at the stage's edge, saying my name,
I had to exist already, my life had to be
Already making its way forward in the world,
For me to have anything to say, to sketch
My predicament, to introduce some key traits,
For me to be granted a wish, for me to wish
To return to my conception, and turn on the lights,

To explain to the disheveled lovers why making me
Was a mistake, I had to exist already.

(*FAERIE, slight, and with incandescent wings,
appears. She carries a child's guitar.*)

FAERIE:

I can make it so you exist, I can grant that wish. But it comes
with a condition.

MAN:

To exist I must exit the stage, is that it? Is that the condition?

FAERIE:

Yes. If you exist, you must use your existence to erase every
worldly trace of yourself. And you must start by exiting this
stage.

MAN:

But what will the audience do, once I've exited?

FAERIE

(strumming the guitar):

At first they will remember you vaguely,
As though your voice were drowned out
By gossipers at a cocktail party,
And with it, the details of your plot—

Then they will hear only rumors of you,
Which, since they seem so bizarre,
They will ascribe to innuendo.
Then only silence where you were.

MAN:

And this process will take how long?

FAERIE:

You will not know until you are finished it.
And when you are finished it you won't know.

MAN:

Why should I be created just to undo my creation?

FAERIE:

This is a common question, and unanswerable.

MAN:

As a child I had a stuffed dolphin. I carried it with me
everywhere. I think what I would like now is a symbol, to
carry around with me in my mind. Can I choose a symbol,
just to make the process easier? I am scared; I think if I had a
symbol, I would not be so scared.

FAERIE

(playing her guitar):

Your symbol is the Ferris wheel, which gobbles
Its own tail, the peaceful circle,

The serene return to origin and out again,
As though the return never happened,

The journey undoing the return,
The return undoing the journey,

The pattern made from the pattern it traces:
A pattern that, by tracing it, it erases.

MAN:

My children loved the Ferris wheel in Paris;
We shared a cramped car
With a piano teacher from Lyon.

You had a feeling that the world was wide,
That people went to such beautiful lengths
To abate each other's misery—

On the Ferris wheel, I can remember thinking,
How odd that I am thinking,
Not about the Paris skyline

(Which I had never seen, though I was thirty-nine)
But about the Paris Ferris wheel,
A principle of human self-obsession

That often feels, to me, dangerous,
But at that moment, riding the Ferris wheel,
Not at all interested in the Champs, or Notre Dame,

It felt like an affirmation of what is really human.
I thought of community theater, for some reason.
I had a deep wish that someday

My boys would play
Clara in a drag version of *The Nutcracker.*
The weird things people do to make each other happy—

Not each other, no—to make the human race
Average out happy, so we break even,
In the long run, with pain. And my children smiling

Beside me. And the piano teacher took our picture.
We represented, to her, what she
Represented, to us: some potential breadth

In human empathy, a break from the loneliness
Dated midcentury plays describe, a way
To think of children without sentimentality

And, more important, of strangers
Just as they are, in a shared
Ferris wheel car, and without metaphysical cliché.

FAERIE:

Empathy is hard; it paralyzes people.
You should indulge it only occasionally.
The result is the same either way.
Your work must be tireless—and even,
I am sorry, a little pitiless.

MAN:

So now I must exit the stage.

FAERIE:

Now you must exit the stage.

(*MAN* hesitates a moment.)

(*FAERIE* starts weeping uncontrollably, her tiny body heaving
in deep sobs, as she repeats, "I'm sorry, oh god, I'm sorry" in
a voice the audience suddenly realizes is intimately familiar
to the man. The man comforts her awkwardly. It is as though
they have known each other for many years, as though this
were the culmination of many moments between them. The
man is torn between his desire to comfort his dear friend and
his wish not to appear to the audience to know her personally.
As her sadness deepens, his self-consciousness grows. Now
everyone, surely, can see that they are lovers. He wishes they
could perform the entire play over, from beginning to end. He
can see that he broke character; he thinks that if he can stay
in character himself, maybe this once he could keep her in
character. He wishes to start the play over.)

(*FAERIE* grants *MAN* his wish.)

(The stage goes dark.)

(The lights come on.)

(An empty stage. *MAN* stands on the front of the stage.)

*

FINIS

Arm in Arm

After Remy Charlip

Echolalia

I am my father's son
I am my father's
Son I am
My father's son
I am

Echolalia

Isn't it better to be in the game saying "Isn't it better to be
in the game rather than on the sidelines" rather than on the
sidelines saying "Isn't it better to be in the game rather than
on the sidelines"?

Circular Song

O Hell
Hell O
Bye Good
Good Bye

No Poem

No rain.
No thought.
No candle.
Nobody came in from the rain.
Nobody thought the thought.
Nobody lit the candle.
No water.
I am thirsty.

I Want

A plate
With a spider on it
Holding a plate
With a toad on it
Holding a plate
With a fish on it

Two Wrongs

Nobody said
Nobody said

I said
Nobody said

Nobody said
I said

Nobody said
Nobody said

Interrogative

In the boughs of the tree
Is a monkey
Is a monkey
In the boughs of the tree?

Echolalia

I am my son's father
I am my son's
Father I am
My son's father
I am

3.

Bicentennial

Box and One

Here is our box and one:
The crucifix

An ice pick in the back
Of the wily point guard trooper's son.

Our press owes everything to Christ,
Our swish is the blood of sacrifice.

Last week we fucking killed St. Paul!

We're on defense inside my head.
The little synaptic me, No. 5
Guards a little synaptic forward

Inside the exact simulacrum
Of the Old Gym, eons later,
Now gooey with my brain matter—

And now the forward posts
And plants his feet—
Eureka! I had this thought:

To get a girl to flash her breasts
From her back patio,
First hold her cat hostage—

Then threaten the cat with fireworks
Aimed straight at its head . . .
So that was puberty: caught cat.

A pivot, another pivot, a pick—
He plays me tight
But I have my elation as my guide;

I have won not just any game;
A Cieplicki congratulates me.
I'll be in the Hall of Immortals.

I'll be immortal in the memory of men;
For writing poetry, I'll be
The poet equivalent of a Cieplicki.

(All rabbits in my poems are based
On an actual rabbit I caught,
Cognoscente of Centennial Field

And thick ravine, never
The transparent eyeball,
Ever the perv of Colchester Ave.)

What Thigpen wrought
Thigpen got

Linebacker
Southerner

Surrounded by rhymes
Inside this poem

Now he hides
Inside the void

Who lassoed me
Dim, kind, and drunk

Now I'm out of bounds.
Ten souls, numbered
And not one of them is me—

I try to inhere inside
A kayak bound
For Juniper Island

But find, instead, my psyche
In a mini-bonsai
In a wrecked terrarium—

(The cat was a Japanese maple;
The girl was my right fist;
The firecrackers were Seth's, anyway—

Nothing I say is true
Nor is it wrong to say
It's wrong to say—)

My grandfather had a depth finder,
He could find any walleye
In the breakwater of the lake,

It worked by radar no sonar
No Kevlar no Mylar
No anger no prayer

One day a walleye appeared
Upon the deck of his boat—
A sign from God, and edible—

That weekend's game I had
The calm of the elect,
As I smashed Christ the King

With my inimitable foul shot
And later feasted
On the oracle, Ore-Ida.

A sign from God who said:
Daniel, go inside
In the back of your black-lit closet

And commune with a magazine
And, lo, some later you
Years after, in the middle
Of his life's journey

Will peer over your shoulder
And wonder what it's like
Inside the inside of the cover girl.

Ten souls, numbered.
Instinctively they play
The roles my memory assigns.

The wily one is always Hanzas.
It's always Aguiar's temper,
The jump shot effloresces

Every time inside Lorenz's palm—
Ten souls and there I am—
No there, the shivering one,

St. Johnsbury: I'm sidelined;
I ventriloquize whatever man I become;
I emote like a hawk.
My vantage point is treetops, prey.

Whatever I see, you see—

I have my famous throb already on!

Where Are They Now?

The Pompeians are having their term abroad.
The astronauts pray for an iron spider.
A fire hose blasted the bumblebee to pieces.
The hurricane spared the life of John Keats.
The hockey captain was overtaken by disease.
The Pompeians are the delight of children everywhere.
She took off her parka and the rest is X-rated.
Imagine the surprise on the face of that bumblebee:
Reality arrived on another scale entirely.
The iron spider turns out to be a flying Eiffel Tower.
Captain, you looked thin at Thanksgiving.
The Pompeians recline enormously above the Pike.
A Siberian with a hard-on plans the Mastodon's encore.

Algebra

A reggae concert at a Jesuit college in Korea:
The band is Taiwanese, the man, Canadian;
His wife, a Filipina, is mistaken for Hawaiian
By the band, four Taiwanese men with dreadlocks,
Who keep on buying the raucous table mojitos,
Even the Dean, who sojourned as a policeman
In Boston, during the busing crisis—
Many young men in that era, of our class,
He tells the partyers, had reason to hate the lazy . . .
And now the Canadian, who is my father, though
I am on the other side of the planet
Learning algebra, says to them yes, America
Was a place back then you tried, we all tried
To get away from, get as far from it as possible—

Bicentennial

1.

Moving as a mind moves across a math problem,
Or an eye across a lover's body,
Or a dragonfly across the sky,
Or history, through wars and bodies,
Or a film from frame to frame,
Or the moods, strangers to each other,
Or a ferry across a lake all day,
Move with me now, for I need company—

I have this wish to get caught up in something
Precisely unlike a poem, unlike writing
For its straightforwardness, its power
That is not the power of half-secrecy
But is, instead, something enormous
And potentially dangerous, and this is all
I am afraid will move my mind one inch
Off the small white tee where it sits and waits.

My mind sits on its small white tee and waits
For something like what others experience
When they avert a tragedy, but barely,
And all of life is refocused in that moment,
Even the parts they hated yesterday,
Or, worse than hated, felt merely a blank
Where emotion would be, a blank
Where meaning would be if only they

2.

Could find the exact site in Paris, by the Seine,
Where the princess died, and see the spot,
And remember the night she died, late
In New York in the era when my friends and I
Did copious amounts of ecstasy at parties
And when it hit you, you simply shone.
Now everyone in that room was beautiful,
And, in the mirror, your own face was a gift

For which you owed even total strangers thanks.
This was what led you in the first place
To make the call, pool the money, and meet the guy
In an alley off West Fourth Street, returning
To the bar or party with a handful of banana-
Colored pills, heads back, and away we go,
Though that night none of us expected to go
Exactly where we were going that night.

I remember, later, in the standards bar: the weeping men
Who, by some accident of history and their bodies
It happened cared for her the way you would a friend,
And one man requested "Oh Lady Be Good" at the bar,
And the sad slow song rang through the bar
Until I did feel, as the song kept telling me I did,
Like a lonesome babe in the wood, adrift
Upon some serotonin raft in a wide, slow stream

3.

Of time, late, late in the night of my childhood
Before I had done anything yet I would regret.
Now it was 1976, and my body in my bed
Felt for the first time what being part of a country
Feels like, a memory of flags and songs
And foods I'd never had before,
For it was the country's birthday, the country
Was having its birthday party, in a park, by the lake.

What being part of a country felt like, in the park,
With the entire breakwater full of boats,
With ferryboats blaring music offshore,
Everyone acting as though it made them happy
To be part of the country, even those I later learned
Were hippies, including my aunts and uncles,
Whose code seemed to include, toward children,
Kindness, what it felt like being part of a country

Was to be quite specifically targeted for love,
As though a letter from a stranger had arrived
Delivering the best, the most unexpected, news.
A neighbor put me up on his shoulders
So I could see, better, the band concert,
War veterans playing French horn, the neighbor
Who moved to Boston and became a caterer
Before he moved back home into his bedroom

4.

Where his parents cared for him the year he died.
He'd been my babysitter, the only boy
Who ever cared for me, and I remember
His patience in watching me play, for he
Too seemed to have kindness as part of his code,
And when he died the neighbors gathered
In the small front yard and planted a lilac
Which, whenever I visit home, I go and see.

Did you know next door to our house
There used to be a small stained-glass chapel
Attached to a dormitory, where the masses
Had a distinct "folk" flare and kindness
Radiated from the mousy students,
Almost as though it was part of their code?
The girls from Rutland or St. Johnsbury,
Or far away, like Danbury, Connecticut,
Girls that now would be approaching sixty,

Who sometimes cared for me upstairs
In their tidy dorm rooms, with crucifixes
On the corkboard, coffee mugs, and toys
They'd brought with them from home,
Which now they gave to me, so I could play.
And sometimes nuns in the convent,
Whose code, it appeared, included kindness,
Showed me the few things they brought

5.

From home to their small cell-like rooms:
One, a young nun, was a coin collector
And she showed me a Standing Liberty quarter
Engraved with the first initial of a boy
She'd dated, and who'd taken her to the fair;
I had the distinct impression she still loved him,
The way that whole afternoon led up
To her getting the quarter from her drawer,

And putting it on the TV tray
Next to her bed, next to the rosary,
And watched me react when she said
The word *boy*. What does *R* stand for,
Sister? Richard, she said, and I wondered
(Since I was a coin collector, too,
And knew the value of every coin)
How much less it now was worth engraved.

Now she puts the coin into the drawer, and
We move inside my mind to the Paris skyline,
Where an enormous Ferris wheel appears,
Lit by the light it generates, a wheel
That spins and spins nowhere, nowhere,
All night, whether we watch it or not,
And children having their childhoods right now,
This late in time, as though they had to stand in line

6.

Just to be born, get on, and ride, and
From the top they see the sliver of history
Fate is allowing them to see, before
They disembark and scatter, some to joy,
Some to misery, and whether they live
For a hundred years or die, as some have,
Tomorrow, this is the childhood these children
Are having, which is something I remind

My own children, all the time—I say,
You are having your childhood now,
And they say, yes, Daddy, and I say,
Jokingly, but not really, how do you feel it is going,
And they light up and they say, Great
Which is just what I would have said as a kid
If someone—though who would it have been?—
Had asked me this very same question:

You are having your childhood, now;
Today you went to the Bicentennial;
Everyone in the world was there,
And you were there: how does that feel?
That's when I say, brightening, Great,
And wait until later, much later in life,
As they must wait, for the real answer. I am having
My childhood now; that's me; I am at a party

7.

By the lake, the boats jostle for space
Inside the breakwater, a neighbor lifts me
Up to see the band concert, the French horns
Blare, the men wear their war uniforms,
The hippies are riding history, the ferries
Are playing blues for the private parties,
The mountains across the water, that's New York.
I am having my childhood right now

In this country, in 1976, that's me
Near the cannons that point to the Adirondacks,
That's me clapping when the parade
Wends by, I am in a park, by the lake,
This is the exact moment in time when I exist
As a five-year-old, in this country,
And everyone is there, at the Bicentennial,
There's the mayor and the Chamber of Commerce,

And there's the National Guard, and the Rotarians,
And there's my daddy, though he never knew me,
My handsome daddy, happy, dancing the day away,
My tall, handsome daddy and his brand-new family,
Just starting out in life, elated at the thought
They'd made it this far, to this enormous party
The country threw for itself—because who else would?—
One billion years ago, today, on its birthday.

Acknowledgments

Thanks to the following publications, where these poems first appeared:

Harper's: "Interviewing Janet Malcolm"; "Away We Go"

The Harvard Advocate: "One on One," 1; "Inscription"; "Star Catcher"

The New York Review of Books: "Nowhere Fast"

The New Yorker: "Obituary"; "One on One," 3; "Titian v. Roadrunner"; "Opening Lines," 2 (as "The Boy in the Egyptian Wing"); "Father and Son"

The Paris Review: "Bicentennial"

Society: "Vital Signs"

Raritan: "Box and One"

For support in writing some of these poems, thanks go to the Solomon R. Guggenheim Foundation and Wellesley College.

Special thanks to Annie Adams, who reads everything first; to Deborah Garrison, who reads it next; and to Meghan O'Rourke, Deborah Landau, and Darrin Straus, who read the title poem the day it was written, July 21, 2011.

Dan Chiasson is the author of three previous collections of poetry, most recently *Where's the Moon, There's the Moon,* and a book of criticism, *One Kind of Everything: Poem and Person in Contemporary America.* His essays on poetry appear widely. The recipient of a Guggenheim Fellowship, an Academy Award from the American Academy of Arts and Letters, and a Whiting Writers' Award, Chiasson teaches at Wellesley College.

A NOTE ON THE TYPE

This book was set in Celeste, a typeface created in 1994 by the designer Chris Burke. He describes it as a modern, humanistic face having less contrast between thick and thin strokes than other modern types such as Bodoni, Didot, and Walbaum. Tempered by some old-style traits and with a contemporary, slightly modular letterspacing, Celeste is highly readable and especially adapted for current digital printing processes, which render an increasingly exacting letterform.

Composed by North Market Street Graphics
Lancaster, Pennsylvania

Printed and bound by Thomson-Shore
Dexter, Michigan

Designed by Soonyoung Kwon